THE NEW MOM'S GUIDE TO
Your Body
after Baby

THE NEW MOM'S GUIDE TO

Your Body after Baby

Susan Besze Wallace

with Monica Reed, MD

a division of Baker Publishing Group
Grand Rapids, Michigan

© 2009 by MOPS International

Published by Revell
a division of Baker Publishing Group
P.O. Box 6287, Grand Rapids, MI 49516-6287
www.revellbooks.com

Printed in the United States of America

Library of Congress Cataloging-in-Publication Data
Wallace, Susan Besze, 1969–
    The new mom's guide to your body after baby / Susan Besze Wallace, with Monica Reed.
        p.   cm. — (The new mom's guides ; bk. 1)
    ISBN 978-0-8007-3298-1 (pbk.)
    1. Puerperium. 2. Mothers—Health and hygiene. I. Reed, Monica, M.D. II. Title.
RG801.W35 2009
618.6—dc22   2008037949

The information provided herein should not be construed as prescribed health-care advice or instruction. The information is provided with the understanding that the publisher does not enter into a health-care practitioner/patient relationship with its readers. Readers who rely on information in this publication to replace the advice of health-care professionals, or who fail to consult with health-care professionals, assume all risks of such conduct.

Published in association with the literary agency of Alive Communications, Inc., 7680 Goddard Street, Suite 200, Colorado Springs, CO 80920.

Contents

Contents

Introduction

We're in This Together

She sat refreshed after a very necessary shower, her oversized rocker moving gently. Through a picture window she could see snow falling from the gray sky. Holding a new baby couldn't have felt more right, more cozy, more miraculous.

In his sleep he lifted a tiny hand and grabbed her finger. "I am home," he seemed to say.

"I am home," she breathed, glancing at the stack of hospital discharge papers and freebies littering the kitchen table. "Now what?"

That perfect moment is etched forever on my heart. The baby I hoped for, prayed for, and waited for was finally in my arms! No one told me that in the days to follow, the euphoria would fade. There were certainly times of unspeakable joy but also unspeakable physical and emotional realities that left me feeling pretty bewildered. I didn't know how to talk about them.

Bleeding, cramping, feeling exhausted, being sore up here and sore down there, starving—but someone else's appetite now coming first. One day everyone is showering a pregnant woman with questions and advice, holding doors open for her, satisfying her cravings. The next day there's a little person outranking his mom's needs at every turn. A life-giving, taut belly has turned to mush, just like the sleep-deprived brain in the same body.

Did you miss the hospital pamphlet on that too?

On the pages that follow, we will seek to identify some of the stealth issues of the heart, mind, and body you might encounter and be unprepared for after bringing a baby home. The "we" I'm referring to is dozens of moms and mom medical professionals who have been there, moms who wish they'd known some things earlier, moms who wish they'd shared more with their friends and family and not felt so isolated, moms who loved this crazy period in their lives and don't want *you* to go it alone.

Our hope is that you'll gain a new understanding of the challenges you face, see that you are indeed normal, and learn ways to baby *yourself* so you can be at your best as you embark on the privilege of parenting.

Whose Body Is This?

Navigating and Accepting Change

After you've had a baby, you don't come home from the hospital the same person who checked in. Whether you delivered vaginally or via cesarean section, in thirty minutes or two days, you must recover. And that's when the real labor begins.

As unique as your birth story was, so will be your road of recovery. Some women bounce back quickly, while others take weeks. Don't beat yourself up if you can't shake that cruddy feeling. *And don't compare yourself with others.* That will get you nowhere but frustrated fast. While people tend to pepper a new mom with questions: "How's the baby doing? How's she sleeping?" I always try to ask how *mom* is feeling. No one is holding *her*, feeding *her* on a schedule, or easing *her* into soft, new pajamas. But maybe we should!

It's been my experience that women feel they can share only the socially acceptable parts of life after baby with most other women. Usually they stick to the sleep challenges. But there's so much more. We'll get to the emotional ride shortly, but first, some honest thoughts on the gory after the glory of having a baby.

Bleeding

You knew there would be blood involved in childbirth. You may not have realized that *mom* gets to wear a diaper afterward too. The discharge, called *lochia*, is heavier with a vaginal birth than a C-section—having had both, I can vouch for that. It's tissue from the lining of your womb and should turn from bright red to pink or brown and be about finished by the time you have your six-week, post-baby checkup, if not before. But it can feel like it goes on forever. The humongous pads provided in the hospital might seem bulky and bothersome—very institutional—but use them. Take home the extras. You'll change them often enough in the beginning not to care about anything but coverage; plus, six weeks of pads gets expensive. Take home the sexy mesh underwear too. Use it. Take it. Trash it.

When you are breast-feeding, your uterus contracts, and it's likely you will feel gushes of blood when you stand up after, if not during, nursing. You should err on the side of changing your pads too often, just to be ready for these times. Remember that dad will have no idea what's going on inside you as you attempt to feed the baby. I always felt a little reminder was in order. I'm not sure what I wanted him to say, but I'm pretty sure he didn't say it. Really, how could he understand? Still I longed for his empathy.

I said we were going to be honest, right? Well here goes. After my third son was born by C-section two months early, I was hooked up to a catheter, some blood pressure socks, an IV, a pain ball for my incision, and I'm not sure what else. With two young boys at home, my husband was pretty much homebound, and I was pretty much alone. If the white board they use as a pain scale had been within reach, I might have hurled it across the room. I was trying desperately to find a comfortable position for my stapled stomach and get some rest, and suddenly I felt like I had to go to the bathroom—right away. I was like a creature from a bad sci-fi movie, lumbering across the room with all my wires and machinery and three-day-dirty hair. When I managed to pull down and sit down, I thought I would pass out from the pain and loneliness of the moment.

And then my uterus dropped in the toilet. Or so I thought. By then I'd pulled the cord, and a nurse was trying to assess the source of my tears. She assured me that it wasn't my uterus and told me I'd passed a blood clot the size of a grapefruit. Lovely!

I share this for a couple of reasons, neither of which is to frighten you. If you don't feel right about what your body is doing, don't suffer in silence. Call the doctor. Clots are common at home too, though usually not that big. But if you aren't sure, ask. Here's the bigger picture: there are moments after having a baby, in the hospital and at home, that you feel desperately alone, rocked by the physical trauma you've just undergone and the ripple effects it has on your body and spirit. Personally, I think it's preparation for the job ahead. Think how glass is tested and twisted in fire to become beautiful art. I think the first months after the birth of our baby mold us, cultivating our empathy for those who suffer, making us into mothers. It can be a gut-wrenching process, literally.

Not long after that experience, I was comforting my five-year-old on the bathroom floor during a bout of the stomach flu. This time I was the nurse, but I remembered well the tears that come from feeling like your insides are falling out. And I hope I never forget.

Ouch

It hurts to pee. If you delivered vaginally, you will probably have pain caused by stretching, tearing, or cutting. My hospital had a can of Dermoplast, an anesthetic spray, waiting to soothe. It helped (and it works on cuts and scrapes, so I moved it to the kids' first-aid kit when I'd recovered). The hospital also recommended using a squirt bottle of warm water on the vaginal area to dilute the stinging potential of urine. I dreaded how much it hurt to pee, so I waited until the last second. The squirt bottle doesn't help when it's not ready and waiting or the water is cold! But if you can "plan ahead," and bite your lip, it helps.

Feeling Low

Good Advice

Ice packs, best early on.

Pain reliever, as directed by a doctor. *Do not take aspirin if you are breast-feeding.*

Frequent pad-changing.

Warm-water squirt bottle while you pee.

Squeeze your cheeks together as you sit down.

Limit how long you sit still.

Witch hazel compresses.

Sitz baths: shallow warm-water soaks.

Take stool softener as directed and drink plenty of water; don't strain with bowel movements.

Always call a doctor with increased pain or swelling or if you run a fever.

Down Low

If you are afraid to pee, imagine your delight when it's time for number two! Hopefully in the hospital you were given a stool softener to make that experience bearable. Drink water—lots of water.

If you received an episiotomy, a surgical cut to enlarge the baby's exit path, the pain might be a little more intense, but it *will* end. Prolific mom-and-baby author Ann Douglas once said of her own episiotomy: "I can still remember how gingerly I had to sit for weeks after the fact. I perfected the art of sitting at a forty-five-degree angle on one bum cheek because it was too painful to sit in my regular position" (WebMD live interview, August 26, 2003). She advises a hemorrhoid cushion or extra pillows on hand to help assist with a comfortable sitting position.

There were two words the nurses used a lot that I'd never heard before childbirth: *sitz bath.* Easy enough, right? You just *sit* in the bath. Well, apparently a sitz bath is a plastic tub that fits over the toilet and can be filled with a few inches of warm water. Sit for twenty minutes and get relief. I had three children before I knew what the tub was for. I thought it was for toting home all your stuff. They should hand out vocabulary lists with those home instructions.

The second term that caught me clueless was *witch hazel.* It's an herbal remedy that dries and cleanses the skin, an astringent produced from steaming the twigs of a shrub. All you *need* to know is that drugstores sell witch hazel wipes that are very soothing in helping heal your baby exit. And later you can use them on other sores, bruises, swelling, eczema, shaving cuts, insect bites, poison ivy, sunburns, and blisters. Not a bad purchase.

Witch hazel is also helpful for hemorrhoids. *Sigh.* Yes, another lovely reward for carrying another person around for nine months. Hemmies are a frequent result of pushing during childbirth and the pressure we exert when we feel constipated. It's like walking around with highly sensitive grapes between your legs. Only one thing made me feel better when I developed one of these lovelies while pregnant with my second child—empathy. A good friend happened to call me just as I was getting off the phone with a nurse who had advised me, "Just push it back in." I was in tears. I decided to come clean and tell my friend the reason for my sorrow. "Susan," she said, "remember a few months ago when you asked if I was tired or upset? You said I seemed a little sad? *That* was why." She went on to share her travails. It was only then that I knew I'd survive. Beautiful, intelligent, seemingly together people get them too, and live to walk again at a normal pace.

A few more words on dealing with pain. Everyone has a different threshold for discomfort. I know mine expanded greatly after I had kids. Either that or I finally realized that complaining wasn't going to make me feel better! But if

"Those first weeks seemed like a dream world, so fuzzy. I didn't expect the pain."

—Lynda

"I craved going to the chiropractor for a massage during those first six months. I think the combination of recuperating from the C-section, breast weight, feeding and holding the baby was a difficult surprise on my muscles."

—Lisa

you hurt, you hurt. Take your doctor's advice on medication. You are not weak because you need medicinal relief. Also, seek distraction. If nursing the baby is uncomfortable in the beginning, as it often is, have a movie on low volume or play some soothing music or thumb through a magazine. Slowed, focused, and deep breathing also became a great friend of mine in recovering from C-sections. Sometimes pain leads to frustration, which leads to stress . . . and then you find yourself tied up in knots both physically and mentally. I also tended to find a mantra to repeat when I was feeling great discomfort. "This is only a phase" or "Thank you, God, for this baby" helped me get perspective in the midst of the hurt.

Time is your friend here. Take one step at a time. No one is timing your recovery the way they time your contractions. Get rid of the panting and breathe deeply. You're no longer in a sprint; now it's a marathon.

C-ing Is Believing

Could there possibly be a more helpless feeling than lying pregnant and naked on an operating table, being shaved and drugged because your baby, with a dropping heart rate, is about to be swiftly delivered from your abdomen? I knew plenty of women who had had C-sections and seemed nonchalant about it. So I thought there was something wrong with me that, months later, my mind kept replaying the fuzzy trauma of my own experience. I didn't talk about it, but every time I closed my eyes, it was there.

Surgery is no small deal. Our bodies have to recover, and I'd suggest our minds do too. Perhaps you were unprepared for a C-section and disappointed not to finish out a vaginal delivery. Don't let anyone try to whisk away your feelings with one-liners. Yes, the most important thing is that your baby is healthy and here to cherish, but you need to work through your feelings in your own way, your own time.

The Skin You're In

DO . . .

Drink plenty of water to help flush out the toxins of anesthesia and hormones.

Avoid excessive caffeine and soda pop, as it dehydrates and is bad for nursing.

Try alternating hair products to give your hair a boost, but don't expect anything to stop hair loss after giving birth.

Use an astringent to help with oozing pores.

Take warm rather than hot showers and use a moisturizer just after getting out.

Exercise when you are ready. Working up a sweat is good for you!

DON'T . . .

Waste your money in search of an instant over-the-counter solution to skin woes.

Try to open sores or pimples to get the problem "out." Let them heal on their own.

Hesitate to ask for help. Ask your esthetician or hairdresser for substitute products.

Even if you were expecting a C-section, the bright lights of the operating room—and the dim memories anesthesia can cause—can be quite rattling. I kept asking my husband to recount detail after detail for me. I don't even think I knew how fuzzy my memories were until weeks later. Ask your hubby while his are still clear!

And then there's the big achy zipper in your bikini line. Sleeping will be tricky. Prop lots of pillows around you to protect your wound. I found coughing even trickier. Who knew that clearing a slight throat tickle could be so painful? Again, positioning a pillow across your tummy helps. The incision takes four to six weeks to heal; the abdominal wall muscles may take a few months before they are fully healed.

Don't keep looking at your incision. It *will* look and feel better, but early on, it may seem like a purple mess, and bending forward hurts. Motherhood insists that you learn to look at the sunny side of dreary situations, so you might as well start now. It's a battle scar. It's an excuse not to wear a bikini again. Heck, it's an easier way to one day explain to your kids where babies come from. You now have a PG visual aid.

Things we wish we had known? I would have had my husband's hand present to squeeze when the staples were taken out of my incision. For some, it's no big deal, but for me that brief procedure was miserable. It also surprised me that my scar would remain numb in many spots for a long time. A larger issue is this: when doctors and home instructions say to limit your lifting, stair climbing, and exertion, you should. Many women get bursts of energy and think back-to-normal is one load of laundry away. And then they collapse in a puddle of exhaustion because they've done too much too fast. Slow down.

It's worth mentioning that just as you may not realize the major-surgery implications of a C-section, your husband may not either. He might be expecting you to do more than you can, especially if you are trying to! Share with him the instructions that you brought home from the hospital and connect with him regularly on how you're feeling.

Wetting the Bed

Waking up in a wet bed can be a problem too, and we're not talking about the baby here. Night sweats can happen because of the major hormonal changes your body is experiencing. With each child I had, somehow I forgot that I'd wake up in a pool of perspiration, my sheets and pajamas very damp. The first time it happened, I thought my breasts had sprung a leak.

Not much to do here but know that it's a brief phenomenon. Keep a clean T-shirt handy, and ask your husband to change the sheets before they start to smell.

This is as good a place as any to say this: *shower often*. Every bit of ickiness you feel after delivery, after a sweaty night, after a day of nursing, after getting spit up on—all can be helped with a good shower and the fresh start it engenders. Just don't let your C-section incision remain in the shower's path too long early on. Now is a great time to use that sweet-smelling body wash and lotion you've been saving under your sink. As one friend says, "I didn't even need to do my hair or put on makeup. I just felt so much better when I was clean."

Skin and Hair

I wanted to lose weight; instead, I lost hair. I wanted to be full of wisdom, but only my pores were full—of gunk. I wish I'd known how temporary these changes are, but when there's so much going on with your body at once, it's hard to imagine a day when you'll actually enjoy looking in the mirror again.

Both breast-feeding and bottle-feeding mothers lose hair. It grows like a weed during pregnancy, and then it falls out at around three months and up to a year after delivery. A little whisk of the drain with a tissue each day will save you buying a bottle of declogger. Little tufts of hair will sprout again, in some places giving you the look of a child gone wild with scissors. I tried a lot of different shampoos through and after pregnancy, hoping to find the one that would greet my raging hormones with salon-fresh manageability. You might try a product recommended for making your hair feel thicker. But time helps the most.

Stephanie, a hair stylist and mother of three, told me women often impetuously try to do something radical to their hair for a lift of their spirits. "You still feel so fat and ugly and you want a cosmetic change, when what you really need is a change from within," she said. Remember, short hair is less hair to deal with, but if it's a new style for you, it might take just as much time to deal with.

When one of her children was a baby, Stephanie decided spontaneously to get her hair cut at a chain hair salon she'd never been to before. With her hair cut up to her ears in some places due to some bad communication, she left bawling. At home, her husband told her she looked like a pumpkin. Shortly after her bad hair cut, while nursing, Stephanie reached back to what used to be her long, thick hair to find only dried spit-up. That sent her running for another cut—this time for practical not emotional reasons. She went to a recommended stylist this time!

"Think it through. Go gradually shorter or gradually with another color. We don't realize how attached we are to our hair," she says. "And a bad hair day can really send you."

Your skin may also go on strike. For me, nowhere was the hormonal shift more evident. I had an unexplained breakout/rash on my trunk through my pregnancies. I wanted to scrub myself raw, but none of my drugstore purchases did a thing to help. The rash would start at twenty weeks and begin to disappear only when my baby was a couple weeks old—a blip on the calendar, but in the midst of pregnancy and new baby, it seemed like forever. No one could see it, but it affected my self-esteem daily, and I don't think I told a single friend. When I changed clothes, I started avoiding the mirror and hiding from my husband. A dermatologist took an inconclusive biopsy and recommended a very gentle soap. No help. My perinatologist said having the baby was the only cure. Guess it was an early lesson that baby changes everything and we can only control so much.

Acne, worrisome spots, and rashes are the most common reasons for dermatologist visits after having a baby, says Dr. Barbara Reed, a clinical professor at the University of Colorado Health Sciences

Center. "Most rashes are unexplained," Dr. Reed says. "Everyone always wants to know why they got a rash, but it is very, very rare that we can actually tell you that. Everything seems so urgent and different, but don't panic. It makes things worse." Dr. Reed also advises, "Don't expect things to go away overnight. Most skin problems take at least two weeks to get even a little better."

Stretch marks and varicose veins will take much longer to fade or shrink, though sadly they may never disappear completely. A dermatologist can help you consider your options. Retin A, other vitamin A products, chemical peels, and microdermabrasion may help and can be used, even if you're nursing.

It took nine months for your body to get like this. Give it time to bounce back. Facials and massages can help not only your body but your spirit as well. Most of your concerns will soon be distant memories. Work through one problem at a time, and try not to lump your maladies together lest you feel your entire body is betraying you. Your body isn't the enemy; it grew a child for nine months, and it has earned the right to some tender care.

Your Body after Baby
Babying Me

1. The most challenging physical aspect of having had a baby for me right now is . . .

2. These words describe my body and how I feel about it:

3. Whom have I asked for help or advice? Where might I find answers or relief?

2

Breast-feeding Bumps

Being Someone Else's Refrigerator Isn't Always a Picnic

ew mothering issues elicit as emotional a response as breast-feeding. Some women adore nourishing children from their bodies. They love the closeness and dread the end of that chapter of baby's life. Others dread nearly every feeding. They never feel at ease using their body in the process.

According to the National Women's Health Information Center, breastmilk provides the most complete nutrition for your baby, is easier than formula to digest, promotes proper weight gain, and may even lead to children being less overweight later in life. For moms, nursing uses up extra calories, making it easier to lose the pounds

"For me it's always been a *gift* to my babies. But it's almost like God's gift to me. It's precious time with them. I'm able to feed them and keep them going. How rewarding is that?"

Tania

"I never knew nursing was physical and *emotional* for a mom. If someone asked me how I was in those early months, I think my answer depended on how well the baby ate that day—if we were clicking. One day I realized my *mood* had to be my own and that she wasn't responsible for how I felt about nursing. She was learning too."

Sarah

of pregnancy, and lowers the risk of breast and ovarian cancer.

But whatever you know intellectually about nursing, it's normal to be caught off guard physically as you get going. How do you prepare for the sensation of a newborn gnawing at your chest, a lactation expert handling you, or the sight of your body spraying milk four feet away? To be honest, I looked forward to nursing, but just hearing the word *nipple* spoken over and over made me a little uneasy. As one friend put it, "Paying that much attention to any part of my body was a new experience."

It may take a little while before your experience of breast-feeding goes from surprising to rewarding. The contracting of your uterus as you feed your baby is, at moments, an intense cramping. But it's short-lived. Engorgement is what happens when your breasts fill with milk. A woman can go from fretting that she will never have milk come

"My breasts were hard, huge melons. I'll never forget the sight. How are you supposed to nurse? I had to stand under hot water to help soften them. When I was nursing, I hated having my boobs out. I'm modest, so I'd always be in another room and alone all the time. I didn't feel like it was a bonding experience with my baby. I breast-fed for two weeks and detested every moment. A friend of mine mentioned pumping. It was my savior, since for me the most important thing about nursing was the nutritional benefit. By pumping and using a bottle, my baby received the nutrition and I avoided the embarrassment. My second son and I had a totally different beginning. I pumped the whole time."

Angela

in to becoming several bra sizes bigger in just hours. Even well-endowed women can be in awe of their ballooning cleavage. The achy discomfort of engorgement may require patience and warm compresses as your body and your baby work together to determine how much milk is needed for each feeding.

How a woman's body "performs" is probably going to determine in part what appeal breast-feeding has for her. If there is a good milk supply, a comfortable latch from baby to nipple, and limited soreness, it makes a difference. How a woman views her body also plays a role. The practice is universal, but it's also unique to each woman.

"It's invasive, private, maybe a little awkward, but I loved the baby being that close to me," Lisa said. "That's what kept me going."

My friend Denise said she never realized nursing would hurt her nipples at the beginning, "but then I don't even like to pluck my eyebrows!" she said.

I was lucky. I enjoyed nursing, and it came pretty naturally for my kids and me. Even my little two-and-a-half-pounder was a quick learner. I pumped on full power, never got mastitis, nursed each child for nine to fourteen months, and at the end kept telling myself "just one more time" for many more times. It felt natural. I felt needed.

I have also seen my babies sneeze boogies on my breasts; had a houseguest pick up a stray, *used* nursing pad that had fallen out; pumped in a moving car many times; and occasionally felt uncomfortably scrutinized in public for giving my kids the recommended nutritional start in life—even though I was well-covered. It's not always easy.

The decision to breast-feed is your call. Just don't make the call to stop too early. Our entire life changes when we bring baby home. It's amazing he doesn't start crawling immediately to get away

"The first time around, I wish I would have had someone come to my own house—not the hospital room—to help me out. I just got so confused about the whole nursing thing, how much, how often, when do you wake them. You don't realize that getting stressed out decreases your milk. I really tried to put on a happy face, but I just didn't love it."

Jenn

Got Milk?

Lagging milk production can frustrate moms. Contact your obstetrician or pediatrician before taking anything, but consider the following for maximizing milk output.

- Keep on a regular schedule with nursing and/or pumping.

- Drink lots of water.

- Watch your diet and make sure you are taking in the recommended 2,500 calories a day.

- Get rest. Yes, it's tough, but it's essential.

- Assess your stress level. Breasts attached to an uptight mom don't work as well.

from our racing heart and shaky nerves. *Breast-feeding is uncomfortable in the beginning, and you will not get the hang of it in a week.* Your baby is changing enormously, and no two days may seem alike. Nursing changes again when your colostrum, your initial offering to the baby, changes to actual milk during baby's first week of life. It changes the first time you eat something your baby reacts to. It changes when your baby goes through a growth spurt and seems to eat nonstop. It changes with her first immunizations. It changes the first time you are up in the middle of the night and feeding *isn't* the comfort your child is seeking. Try not to lump each circumstance into a nursing-is-too-hard phenomenon. Take one thing at a time and *call those lactation specialists.* Yes, they can come on strong in the hospital, but you were extra-sensitive and all you wanted to do was hold that tiny new mushy person while he slept. Lactation experts have solved countless problems, and they

"Grace was losing a lot of weight in the beginning, and they wanted me to supplement her with formula. I felt so rejected. I had milk but she wasn't taking it, and it made me not like her. I felt so unloved by her, even though I knew I was being irrational. Then one day it was explained to me that when she was nursing forty-five minutes on each side, she got burned out and tired, and the formula was coming without as much effort so she'd take that. I just didn't know what I was doing. I used to be happy to pump so someone else could feed her; then I began not wanting to share her. I got that attachment you hear about, just not at the beginning."

Lynda

want to help you give breast-feeding your best shot. (If the hospital where you delivered doesn't provide such help, call the La Leche League at 1-877-4-LALECHE or visit www.lllusa.org to find support in your area.)

My friend Stacia's milk didn't come in for days. Every day she was on the phone with lactation help from the hospital where she delivered. They suggested she add Ovaltine to the milk she drank, because the malt could help. They reminded her to drink lots of water. Together, they waited.

"If it hadn't been for those ladies and my mom, I might have quit," she said. "I went on to nurse for eight months."

Coming to a Crossroads

Many moms speak of a breast-feeding crossroads they face. It may come at any time, but it brings a moving forward—a comfort level with nursing finally met or an end to nursing efforts. Women stop nursing for different reasons at different stages of baby's life. In the first month or two, baby may not be gaining adequate weight or may not be latching on properly and therefore causing sore spots. At three to eight months, going back to work is tough if the employer is not comfortable with a woman pumping her milk, providing neither the time nor place to do it. At six to nine months, those new baby teeth can put the brakes on breast-feeding for some moms.

Sometimes nursing moms automatically connect bouts of fussiness to nursing and get discouraged—probably far more often than there is an actual food sensitivity at the root of the crying. Yes, there are foods that can affect the milk and cause a baby's fussiness, but every mom-baby combination is different, so there isn't one list of "don'ts" to follow. You may want to consider whether there's a family history of food allergies and eat everything

"I wish someone had told me that underwire bras can increase your chances of mastitis. I was having a fever, sick to my stomach, and still trying to tell myself, No, nothing's wrong with me. Mastitis can definitely make you want to quit nursing, but it doesn't have to."

Jennifer

Whoa Baby!
Making It through Mastitis

What it is. An inflammation of the breast caused by an infection. When milk builds up because of a missed feeding or not being emptied from the breast, it can leak into breast tissue, which can then become swollen and easily infected. Cracked nipples can also allow infection-causing bacteria to get in.

What you'll feel. Fever, chills, body aches, exhaustion, and the infected area will feel warm. More advanced symptoms include swollen lymph nodes in the armpit nearest the infected breast, increased heart rate, and/or a hard, painful lump, which could be an abscess.

What you'll see. A red area on your breast.

What to do. See your doctor, who is likely to prescribe an antibiotic. Take the full course. Keep nursing—it usually helps! Get more rest, drink more fluids, and use cold packs on the painful breast. As your doctor advises, take acetaminophen for pain and ibuprofen to reduce inflammation. Change nursing pads regularly to avoid future infection.

What not to do. Don't get discouraged! You can make it through this usually brief pitfall and can continue nursing successfully. Don't wear your nursing bra too tight and don't wear an underwire bra. Don't skip feeding or pumping sessions.

How to breast-feed. Try a warm, wet washcloth over the affected breast for about fifteen minutes before you nurse to increase milk flow. Massage may help too. Sometimes starting with the unaffected breast will start your milk flowing and make for a less painful nursing session on the other side. Ask a lactation consultant for help if you are worried that baby's latching on or positioning is producing cracked nipples.

in moderation. Chocolate, cow's milk products, and cabbage are common offenders, but many babies handle these just fine. Friends say they had to stay away from oniony salsa. A baby's fussiness that is not accompanied by other symptoms and calms with more frequent nursing is probably not food related. If a breast-fed baby is sensitive to a certain food, she may cry inconsolably for long periods or sleep little and wake suddenly, upset. Other signs of a food allergy include rash, hives, eczema, sore bottom, wheezing or asthma, congestion or coldlike symptoms, red and itchy eyes, vomiting, constipation and/or diarrhea, or green stools containing mucus or blood. Since it can take many days for a food to be completely eliminated from mom's body, sorting out the offending food takes patience. Lactation pros and your pediatrician will help.

Mastitis, a painful inflammation of the breast caused by infection, can be the nursing stumbling

"I had 'overactive letdown' and was told I could have nursed multiples. My baby choked because the milk came down so fast, and she couldn't stay latched for long periods of time. I saw a lactation consultant and even tried the 'Australian hold,' which involved holding my infant on my knee while trying to have her nurse from afar. We had a rough few weeks. Cabbage leaves ended up being my savior! When cleaned and cooled in a Ziploc in the fridge and then placed in my bra, they naturally absorb the milk and ease the pain."

Elizabeth

block. A woman may not know she has it until she's miserable. Usually you start to hurt in one area of your breast. Maybe it's red or warm to the touch. You may feel achy, like you have the flu. But sleep-deprived moms may feel that way anyway! Pay attention to your entire body and check your breasts regularly for hard or hot spots. (It's good practice for the early detection of breast cancer to be in touch with your body this way.)

Sore nipples can also be an aggravation many women don't want to endure. The initial tenderness should gradually go away. If not, poor latching and positioning are likely to blame. The baby is probably not getting enough of the areola into his or her mouth. If it hurts, start again. Ask your doctor or hospital lactation consultant for help if this is a persistent problem.

Here's the thing. *Each of these breast-feeding challenges is very manageable.* You just have to step away from the problem long enough to ask for help and get perspective. Perspective can be hard to come by your first year of parenting—and with each successive child you will likely still be stymied by the crisis of the week. Attitude is everything. If you can endure the ups and downs of breastfeeding, you will give your child a priceless gift, you could lose weight more quickly, you'll save money, and the bonding is worth the bumps.

The Breast Pump

The breast pump can be an amazing bridge between you and your baby, keeping your nutrition close even when you can't be. When you've established a nursing rhythm, introducing a bottle of pumped milk can put one of those night feedings into your husband's hands. It can also allow *you* the flexibility of the occasional bottle when you find yourself in a place where it's tough to nurse. I could always participate in or even lead a meeting if I was bottle feeding rather than nursing. Pumping can help you continue breast-feeding if you go back to work. Pumping milk to leave behind can also allow you to leave the house without feeling like a cow stealing away from the barn.

Speaking of cows, I had no choice but to pump while my preemie son put on enough ounces to be ready for the real thing. I pumped ten times a day early on and every three hours for the forty-six days before he came home from the hospital, and then at home until he had enough energy for all feedings from me. I had thoughts of renaming myself Bessie. It got old. But faithful pumping really does work to increase your milk supply, and you can see the evidence in ounces!

Don't mess around—buy a high-quality pump or rent a hospital-grade machine to get going. Having a picture of your sweet infant nearby when you pump can help stimulate your letdown. There were plenty of moments it felt surreal to pump

"There was a part of me that was really immature because women would just whip it out to feed and I would feel so uncomfortable. Didn't they care that people could see their chest and that they were doing it in public? I had a hard time making eye contact while they were feeding. Now I don't even think twice about it and it's so not a big deal."

Lisa

milk from my breasts. You might not imagine there are other women doing what you're doing. Then one day you'll talk to someone on the phone and recognize the familiar whir of a pump in the background and you'll smile. You will also smile when you have a child old enough to imitate you pumping or commentate races on which side will "win."

A Few Hints

Speaking of sides, I don't know many women who haven't experienced very different milk production from her two breasts. I tried with each kid not to favor nursing on the right, but I did and was a little lopsided as a result. Never fear, you return to normal eventually. For women who leak on one side while nursing on the other, quality pads to slip in your bra are a must. Many women I spoke with said they tried all brands and came back to the ones with an adhesive strip to connect the pad and your bra and prevent the strays I mentioned earlier. Washable pads are certainly comfortable but never seemed as absorbent to me and quickly smelled. I don't mention products by name lightly, but Lilypadz are a fairly revolutionary addition to the marketplace that could save you time and trouble. They are breathable silicone breast pads that really function more as a second skin. You can wear them swimming or with an evening dress, as they stay put while inhibiting leakage. Many times in mothering, women will struggle with a product or an issue, only to find out later that someone has already invented just the thing to make life a little smoother. Don't suffer! Explore!

Who imagines that when she has a baby she'll spend the next year sleeping in a bra? Yuck. It's hard enough to feel like your day is now a wakeful twenty-four-hour cycle of feedings. When I get in bed I want to feel "free," not as though I were too tired to undress. But every time I tried to go braless, I'd regret it and create more laundry. The best compromise was a nursing tank top—or any tank with a nice shelf in it. Adhesive breast pads usually stay put, and you can feel together without feeling strapped in. There's also an Australian-made nighttime tank called the Booby Bib, which is like pajamas and breast pads all in one. If the rave reviews are accurate, the sixty-dollar price tag might be worth it.

Whether you wear one at night or not, good bras are a must. Many women try cheapies and go through them quickly. It wasn't until my third child that I invested in something that didn't look like a sterile straitjacket (think 1950s insane asylum). Again, nice things were out there; I just didn't realize it. Amazing what a pretty nursing bra will do for one's self-image at such an emotionally precarious time. Just remember not to put any bras in the dryer. It hastens their demise.

The Rules of Engagement

As we consider nursing and undergarments, a few thoughts on the rules of engagement. Try to be discreet when nursing in public. It can be done. Often my first son looked like he'd spent an hour in a sauna when he emerged from under a blanket. He spent a decent part of his infancy looking sweaty, disheveled, and bewildered, though full. By my second child I learned that, yes, a baby blanket is great for privacy, as the baby gets latched on, but those smaller square silky blankies, usually more for baby's comfort than keeping him warm, are a lighter drape over a baby's head and his dinner. I'm talking about the ones I thought were a cute but impractical gift and looked more like a doll-size blanket. Two of my children used these blankies for years for nighttime comfort. Practical indeed!

I have nursed everywhere from church to a fancy Valentine dinner in Washington, D.C. I

"My good friend told me that she couldn't believe that I wasn't going to be breast-feeding my daughter. She said I was going to have **big issues** with her getting sick all the time because breast-fed babies don't get sick and bottle-fed babies do. **It hurt my feelings,** and I held on to that resentment for a year. My daughter actually didn't get sick until she was thirteen months old."

Lisa

The New Mom's Guide to Your Body after Baby

did not sit around with my shirt unbuttoned. No one saw my breasts. My kids didn't slurp loudly like puppies at a puddle. I was not out to make a statement. I was just trying to feed my kids what the American Academy of Pediatrics says is best, as well as having a life in the meantime.

Kelly, a registered nurse and lactation consultant, told me she never nursed her first child in public. "I was afraid of being indiscreet. Everything I did, I timed around when he needed to eat—I wouldn't even feed him *at* the doctor appointments but before," she said. "I was very uptight about it all. It was something I didn't think about beforehand and should have."

And this is someone very used to body parts and babies and moms nursing in front of her! Kelly said a couple things changed her attitude. She began noticing other nursing moms in public. She had a second child and had to loosen up. And she even discovered something called a "Hooter Hider," a hip and lightweight cover with an adjustable strap that goes around mom's neck with a rigid collar for peering in and seeing what baby is up to.

"With the second child I just had to be more flexible," she said. "I was so much more relaxed and had so much more freedom. I wish I had discovered that with my first child."

Seeking solitude as you are trying to get the hang of nursing is not only normal, it's best. You want to stay relaxed as you are trying to establish your baby's feeding. As I was finding my rhythm with little Zach, my sister-in-law came to visit. She wanted to go shopping one day. I have long admired many things about Lori's parenting, so I trusted that if she thought "getting out" was do-able, it probably was. I can still remember finding a mall bench, and then a department store lounge, and then a dressing room, and feeding my baby through the day. I expected that every eye in the mall would be on me, but the truth was that most people never even knew I was nursing a child. It was perhaps the finest baby gift anyone gave me: the knowledge that my breasts and my baby and I were not confined to the house. It opened up our whole world. Actually I think it helped me develop a can-do, even adventurous attitude with my kids as to what was possible for us as a team.

When Kelly visits new moms in the hospital, she suggests they nurse in front of a mirror, to see what other people see when they watch. What an awesome idea for increasing your confidence!

When a baby starts to kick and look around while nursing, usually at about seven months, you *will* need privacy. A baby's sudden distractibility can make you think she isn't interested in you or your milk. In truth, she is just waking up to the sights and sounds of the world, and all the stimulation—TV, siblings, you opening mail over her head—can make it hard for her to focus. At that point, intentionally seeking quiet and stillness might be a good idea.

If You Decide to
Bottle Feed
Exclusively...

- Wear a well-fitted support bra.
- Place an ice pack under each armpit to help decrease swelling and pain.
- Take pain medicine as prescribed.
- Avoid running hot water over your breasts.
- Avoid frequent touching or handling of your breasts.
- Engorgement usually goes away in a few days. There are no safe medicines to "dry up" the milk.

Similac Welcome Addition Club
and moms who have been there

I should say here that to the last day of nursing, my husband was concerned with propriety. I think he always imagined that the baby would throw a leg up, blankets would fly, and a boob would be on public display to the gasps of hundreds of onlookers. As my comfort level grew with each month and each child, so did his. He learned to request a booth when we were out to eat or let me have the window seat on a plane. He learned to tug the privacy blanket back over my shoulder when it started to droop without me having to say a word.

Your husband's support of breast-feeding is important. Occasionally he can be *too* supportive. As one friend told me, her husband's pressure to nurse at all costs led to an ultimate "It's my body!" argument between them. But more often, a man can feel set aside as his new child *requires* mom every three hours. Attitude is everything for both of you. Watch how you ask for things—water, a footstool, that extra pillow—while you nurse. Don't be demanding, just encouraging. Let dad burp, change, and swaddle the baby—and be sure to compliment his technique. Lots of moms say that when dad brings a hungry baby to them at night, it is a huge help, and the child feels daddy's secure arms "rescuing" him from hunger. When dad uses a bottle of pumped milk for that middle-of-the-night feeding, he is wonderfully appreciated by all! My husband loved the excuse to cuddle the baby *and* catch up on a little taped TV. For me it took a little effort to *let* dad help. It was hard for me to realize that I wasn't the only one who could care for our new boys. It's easy, when you are finding your way, to hide your own insecurities under the guise of "I must do it all." Think about it.

Please don't judge another mom's decision to nurse or to bottle feed, not even in the deepest part of your heart or mind. Whatever her reasons—maybe medical necessity—each mother has to decide for herself. As you probably know by now, motherhood is highly personal. But it is also a sorority of hope and fear and heart-wrenching desire to do the job "right," whatever that is. You do a disservice to this sisterhood any time you elevate your own choices over some-one else's. Children inspire enough guilt on their own without moms dispensing it to each other. Understanding instead of judging the choices your contemporaries make is not only nice, it's smart. A good mom gathers information from a range of sources, sorts through it, and then does what's best for her own family.

Your Body after Baby
Babying Me

1. What are my feelings about breast-feeding?

2. If I am breast-feeding, what do I like about it? What am I having trouble with?

3. If I have chosen to bottle feed, am I comfortable with my decision?

4. What words describe my body and how I feel about it?

5. What unanswered questions do I have about the way my body is recovering from delivery?

6. Whom have I asked for help or advice? Where might I find answers or relief?

3

Coming Out of the Closet

Weight and Clothes

After you have a baby, your closet is like a boxing ring. On one side hang those tents and T-shirts you're sick of and those pants with a pouch you don't feel you should wear or should need to wear, even though they might be all that fits. On the other side hang pre-baby fashion, favorite shirts that just don't look right over the balloons that are your breasts, and jeans . . . ah, the old jeans. In the middle is you, bouncing from side to side, perhaps throwing a couple of air punches in frustration. There's no clear winner, and your self-esteem can be quickly knocked out.

How to Cope

When we have so little control—over our bodies, our baby's sleep, our emotions—a relatively small thing, like not being able to wear what we want, can often put women over the edge. Be patient. Be gentle with yourself. Remember how you thought nine months would last forever, and then *boom*, it was over? Same with your weight and wardrobe. If you try on the same clothes every day in hopes that pounds were lost in the night, you are setting yourself up for failure and frustration. This is true too if you do a daily weigh-in.

One friend rids her closet of all the things she can't wear post-baby and puts them in the closet of a spare room. One day a month she lets herself try on her old favorites.

When I had little A.J. two months early, I had to go home without him. One of the first things I did was take the two seasons of bought and bor-

"Having to continue to wear maternity clothes contributed to an ugly, grungy feeling I had in the months right after baby. I felt like a sack of unwanted flesh. It surprised me that every part of my body was affected by pregnancy. I couldn't believe how much weight stuck around months later. But I was equally surprised at how my body repaired itself when I gave it care and priority. After a year I was nearly back to my pre-baby weight."

Lisa

rowed maternity clothes and make a pile of them on my closet floor. When my sister asked what she could do to help, I answered, "Get a tub." For me, putting away the maternity clothes was a very important step in completing something, controlling something, and finding order in something during those early days after he was born. I survived in drawstring pants and the very biggest of my old stuff—often left unbuttoned.

Nursing moms have the special challenge of wearing clothes that fit and are flattering but that can be pulled up or aside at a moment's notice to free a breast. I can't tell you how many times I put something on only to realize I'd have to practically get naked to feed a baby. And oh, the sweaters! They seem a good, comfy choice, but they can turn both you and your baby into a sweaty mess when you nurse. After a while, choosing the appropriate thing to wear will become second nature.

"Clothes will never fit the same.
I weigh now what I weighed pre-babies,
but I have plenty of clothes that don't fit
around the waist. My husband just said,
'Doesn't everyone have a pouch?
Don't you just ?'"

Angela

Most men will never so quickly gain and lose as much weight as moms do. It's hard for them to understand many things about the postpartum mind and body, especially the pouch—the dunlop (as in, when you're done it lops over)—the muffin top. How yummy. Men call their extra middle "love handles," and they rarely come with the emotional baggage of giving birth. Accept that when you go on closet tirades, your husband will try to be helpful or remain silent. You might find his silence frustrating, his words empty, and his assurances about your body ridiculous. He means well, and in my experience, he means what he says. So don't take your fashion frustration out on your husband.

And don't take it out on your checking account. Quickly buying new clothes to fit your new—and temporary—body isn't usually a good idea. If this is your first baby, you have no idea what the first year holds for your weight and waistline. And you don't

"I remember getting ready for a football game after having my daughter, and as time went on, I was so aware of my fat hanging over my pants, **that I just had an all-out temper tantrum.** I actually hit my fists on the ground and yelled, 'I am so gross!' **It was good to let it out.** I got some perspective. My weight defined my *self-esteem.* It shouldn't but it did, **and realizing that was good for me."**

Jenn

want to end up with a bunch of too-big things you bought on impulse. As you will one day tell your children, make good choices. That's not to say treating yourself to a little something new and lasting—new underwear was always my favorite—won't give your self-esteem a little boost. A fashionable warm-up suit in cooler weather is a sound choice, and some new shoes may be a necessity, not just a treat. (See "Meet Your New Feet" on pages 92–93.) One friend told me that, after six months in maternity clothes, the thought of continuing to wear them got her so depressed that she finally broke down and bought some bigger things, and then cut off the tags so the size wasn't staring at her. She kept working off the weight, but having some new things to wear was important to her self-image.

You have to decide what's best and most motivating for you. But remember that the body you have after giving birth is not the body you will have a year later.

Creative
Camouflage:
What to Wear

❋ Low-on-the-hip fashions (not crack-revealing teenage wear) are very forgiving to a mushy middle. But wear them with long shirts that cover you completely. Pants that come to the waist will make your tummy feel squeezed in like a section of a balloon animal.

❋ Bigger breasts are often better off with a modest V-neck than a crew-neck style of shirt. A piece of jewelry can be a nice point of interest other than your cleavage.

❋ Nursing shirts got poor reviews from the women we talked to. They're a great idea, but not usually practical or flattering.

❋ That said, remember nursing when you dress. Our moms found knits more practical than button-up shirts because of the stretch factor. Many dresses will have to wait.

❋ Try wearing skirts to feel more feminine and to push yourself out of sweats occasionally.

❋ Avoid overalls unless you farm. They are too forgiving and will not motivate you to get back in shape.

❋ Keep the silk shirts in the dry cleaning bag. You are entering an era in your life of unbelievable goo. Spit-up and drool and drops of medicine and leaky breasts all demand washable fabrics.

❋ Dark colors are slimming. Need we say more?

❋ If something barely fits in the morning, it won't fit at all later in the day. Be comfortable from the get-go and avoid unnecessary frustration.

Losing the Weight

Of course the big question is, how long will it take for these pounds and inches to go away? You have water weight, breast weight, and body fat to deal with. Water goes first, and breast weight will likely take months. And yes, some women never get back to exactly the way they were.

Sylvia Brown, author of *The Post-Pregnancy Handbook*, says that skinny moms who gained thirty to thirty-five pounds lose most of their pregnancy weight in the first three months. Borderline overweight, older moms, or third- or fourth-time moms who gain between thirty-five and seventy-five pounds lose most of their weight between the third and sixth month. Overweight moms will lose most of their excess weight six to nine months after childbirth. (From an interview with Brown on Storknet.com, http://www.stork net.com/guests/postpregnancyhandbook.htm.) I

"I gained eighty pounds. **Eighty pounds!** I ate whatever I wanted and thought, *I'm a runner. I'll run it off.* You hear so much about losing weight breast-feeding. I was down to needing to lose about forty-five pounds, and I was running hard. **I felt like I was in someone else's body.** I ended up shattering a disc on my spinal cord and having surgery with a four-month-old at home. **I did too much, too soon.**"

Kelly

Getting Your Complex Carbs

Best Sources:

bran
wheat germ
barley
maize
buckwheat
cornmeal
oatmeal

Good Sources:

pasta
brown rice
potatoes
other root vegetables
peas
beans
lentils
corn
yams
oatcakes
whole grain pita, brown, or bagel breads
whole grain breakfast cereals,
    like Shredded Wheat
high-fiber breakfast cereals, like All-Bran
old-fashioned oats
Muesli, without added sugar

repeat these numbers only to reinforce that every woman is different, and it takes everyone time to lose weight.

Your average new mom should take in about 2,000 calories a day. A nursing mom should be eating 2,500 calories—including extra protein—because she burns 750 calories feeding the little one. You won't get the weight-loss effects of breast-feeding until about four months. That's when the level of the appetite- and milk-stimulating hormone prolactin settles down, and your retained fluid has made an exit, but your metabolism is still rocking.

So it's important not to use nursing as an excuse to eat a bag of Oreos in one sitting. If you want to maximize your weight loss, make half your calories complex carbohydrates. Sadly, these are not found in Oreos but in whole grain form, such as whole-grain breads, oats, and brown rice. These break down more slowly and give you a steadier stream of energy throughout the day. Simple, refined carbs found in processed, convenience foods tend to be devoid of these natural nutrients and are more likely to be converted into fat and stored.

It's a challenging transition to go from eating ice cream at 10 p.m. to wanting to lose weight fast. Most nursing moms I know get surprisingly, intensely hungry as they keep pace with an infant's needs. Prolactin, which stimulates milk production, also stimulates your appetite. Out-and-out dieting is not advised when you are nursing, but this can be a time when you learn to eat healthier. It always seemed my baby and I got hungry at the same time. His appetite always came first because I felt so guilty listening to the crying! And then I learned how to make lunch and nurse simultaneously. (Yes, this did involve mustard on my son's head once or twice—perhaps that's why he has an aversion to it.) One mom I know made herself

"I was asked a few months
after the birth of each of my girls,
'When are you due?'
That can make you stop
wearing tight-fitting clothes
for *weeks*."

Elizabeth

"Isn't it interesting
how delivering such
a beautiful thing
can wreak overall
havoc
on your body?"

Jennifer

Meet Your
New Feet

Stacey's husband knew something was up. They were at a restaurant with their three-month-old.

"Go ahead and go before we leave. I'll wait."

"Wait for what?"

"For you to go to the ladies' room."

"What makes you think—?"

"You look like you're walking on eggshells, like you are about to burst."

She did burst, into a laugh-cry combination he'd gotten used to these last weeks.

"My feet are killing me! I love these shoes! My feet got fat! I don't know why. My life will never be the saaaaaaame!"

It's true. Your feet are also not what they were before baby.

They balloon because of fluid retention, or edema, during pregnancy. We soak them, we prop them, but the pregnancy hormone relaxin is also at work, loosening ligaments in the feet, causing our twenty-six foot bones to spread. It's the same phenomenon that allows baby to enter the world through your loosened pelvis. While we're quite happy for that, the snug shoe phenomenon can surprise us with the discomfort it causes.

Though the swelling abates after baby arrives, any bone spreading is here to stay. And so is the resulting half- or whole-size increase in shoe size. If you can look at the sunny side of things, you get to buy new shoes! But there are likely some old standbys and Friday-night favorites in your closet that you'll try again and again, hoping their tight fit is all in your head until you limp home, pledging to get rid of them. (Your Friday nights will change dramatically too, but we won't go there yet!)

Don't suffer or cause calluses or bunions to form by denying the reality of your foot size. You were probably already guilty of that before you had a baby, right? Give the too-tights to a good friend. And if you plan to have more children, remember, your feet may not be finished growing yet.

a sandwich during breakfast to have ready at a moment's notice. It kept her from dragging the Doritos bag to the couch for a quick fix while she fed her daughter.

Check out local fitness classes that you and your baby can take together. Walk to the grocery store with the stroller to get exercise and an errand done at the same time. Do crunches on the floor as your baby (safely) has tummy time on or next to you. I know you are exhausted, but it doesn't get much easier to exercise than in your baby's first sleepy months. And it will help the fog to lift. As baby gets more active, and certainly with successive children, scheduling exercise only gets more challenging.

When someone says, "You're looking great!" they mean it. But you know what baby "souvenirs" you have acquired and may even scoff at the compliment. The same is true when you look at others and marvel that they are back in jeans or seem unscathed by housing a baby for nine months. From labor to weight loss to child rearing, remember: everyone has their *stuff*, their issues. You might not know what they're dealing with. So don't compare or set yourself up to somehow feel less successful. Take care of your life-producing body, and accept that it is neither what it was nor what it is yet to be.

Your Body after Baby
Babying Me

1. What am I wearing right now? What would I like to be wearing?

2. What have I eaten today? Am I indulging, binging, being smart, eating enough?

3. Do I have a friend or family member I'm able to laugh and talk honestly with about my new body?

4. What's been my past experience with exercise? What are some goals I can set for getting moving with my new baby?

Downpour

Weathering Your Emotional Storms

Before I had children, I hosted a few baby showers and attended several others. They were sweet, sugary affairs that oozed cute clothes and small talk. I enjoyed them and soaked up every second of the one thrown for me. Okay, maybe the baby food tasting was over the top, but I felt incredibly loved and special that day. And I simply couldn't wait to meet my son.

Hindsight is, to be honest, a little frustrating. At my shower, no one said anything remotely truthful about those first months as a new mom. I had no idea tears would spring to my eyes with only a few seconds' notice after a perfectly fine day. I had no idea the toll of sleep deprivation. I'd been

"I remember my husband talking about how cool the birth of our son was, what the placenta was like and all these details, and I'm thinking, I hated every bit of it. How come I didn't think it was so wonderful? I felt guilty I didn't love it more. And I wasn't about to share that!"

Kelly

"I always ask friends, 'Have you had your big breakdown yet?' You have to have one, if not more than one."

Elizabeth

to college—how bad could a few all-nighters be? I'd been in bad moods. They lift, right? I knew motherhood would change my life, but no one told me it would affect just about every decision I'd make every second of every day.

Since then I've attended baby showers and, no, I didn't corner the new mom to say, "Buckle up, babe. You have no idea what's about to hit you." I guess I'm now part of the conspiracy. Every woman deserves those blissful premotherhood days, when buying tiny clothes and deciding what color to paint the nursery are her foremost concerns. She shouldn't try to guess the first time she will dissolve in a puddle of unexplainable tears, any more than she should worry about her unborn baby's first fever. But I can't help thinking that if more women were more open, more forthcoming about the emotional side of having a new baby, maybe we'd all be a little more prepared when it's our turn. That's my hope here, to explore the range of reac-

"My son has a scar on the top of his cheek from the scalpel they used to cut me open. That's how fast it had to happen. It was that bad, and they told my husband they weren't sure if I was going to come through or not. My son loves hearing the story of his 'battle wound.' I got a lot closer to God at that moment. I came out of it thinking, I've been given a second chance. And yet it's still hard to talk about."

Stacia

tions to having a new baby *before* they take you by storm. It's harder to see the rain, or remember where you keep the umbrella, when it's already pouring on your head.

The Drizzle

The emotional aftershocks of having a baby start right away—and so does trying to suppress them. No matter how much you think you've prepared, the reality of pushing a human being out of your body, or delivering one by C-section, is overwhelming. This is true even without circumstances like the cord wrapped around baby's neck or your barely making it to the hospital in time.

From the first squeak your baby makes, the focus is now on her. You are left in wide-eyed wonder about what you've just done—delivering your wonderful baby—but the trauma and the pain that you experienced is eye-opening as well. You'd like to talk about these things, but it's pretty personal and you're not sure if anyone is really interested.

You need to find someone who will listen, a sibling or friend who cares and will listen to you. This was your birth day, not just baby's. We recover from trauma by talking about it and releasing it. My dear friend Kristin's exciting labor and delivery happened before her husband made it to the hospital. A friend of hers captured the details of the day and wrote up the story of Jake's birth as a priceless gift. She said it helped her process the process. She passed on that tradition to me, chronicling my youngest's ten-week-early arrival with every detail she was privy to and presenting it to me on his baptism day. She had listened to my ramblings attentively, and helped me make sense of and make plans after his premature birth. Because it was a fuzzy and fast-paced week in the hospital for me, her gift helped all of us hang on to something I might have otherwise eventually lost.

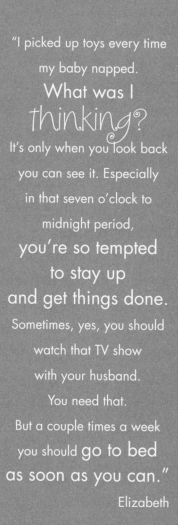

"I picked up toys every time
my baby napped.
What was I
thinking?
It's only when you look back
you can see it. Especially
in that seven o'clock to
midnight period,
you're so tempted
to stay up
and get things done.
Sometimes, yes, you should
watch that TV show
with your husband.
You need that.
But a couple times a week
you should **go to bed**
as soon as you can."

Elizabeth

Believe it or not, even awesome memories fade. Whatever your opinion of journaling or your insecurities about how you write, consider taking time to record the details of your child's arrival. It will be cathartic for you, your child will love to hear the story over and over, and one day it will be a priceless treasure that is passed on, as your kids have kids of their own.

Disappointment is another emotional aspect of life for new mothers that isn't often verbalized. Who on *earth* could be disappointed with a new baby? I'm not talking about go-back-in-you're-not-cute-enough disappointment. I'm referring to letdown, when the expectations of having a baby and the reality don't immediately line up and you feel down. Maybe you had a C-section when you wanted to go natural. Maybe labor happened before you were ready, and you feel a little cheated. Maybe you were a fertility patient and had worked so long at achieving and sustaining a pregnancy that now having the baby instead of *trying* to have one leaves you feeling a little lost. Perhaps it's your last baby, and you had your tubes tied, and there is some grief, or sense of loss, invading your joy. You might also simply miss the feeling of having your child inside you. You are not alone.

There's no "right" way to feel after having a baby. Your mind and your heart were as busy changing as your uterus was during those nine months. Usually these feelings will abate quickly. Talking to your husband, doctor, or friends is key. Sometimes just talking about these "unmentionables" can help clarify what you are feeling and then free you to move on.

The Clouds

Ever put Windex in the refrigerator or ice cream in the pantry? Ever gone frantically looking for

Tips for
Good Napping

The right length:
A short nap is usually recommended (20–30 minutes) for short-term alertness. This type of nap provides significant benefit for improved alertness and performance without leaving you feeling groggy or interfering with nighttime sleep.

The right environment:
Your surroundings can greatly impact your ability to fall asleep. Make sure that you have a restful place to lie down and that the temperature in the room is comfortable. Try to limit the amount of noise and the extent of the light filtering in. While some studies have shown that just spending time in bed can be beneficial, it is better to try to catch some zzz's.

The right time:
If you take a nap too late in the day, it might affect your nighttime sleep patterns and make it difficult to fall asleep at your regular bedtime. If you try to take it too early in the day, your body may not be ready for more sleep.

Source: National Sleep Foundation

your keys only to find them in your left hand? Sleep deprivation slowly, insidiously clouds your concentration, your decision making, your everything. And it makes you more prone to depression.

It's so subtle. You know you're tired. You know how much sleep you got last night. But you are up, dressed, living life, feeding baby, cooking meals, functioning. You may be having a conversation and suddenly you can't find the next word of your sentence. You criticize yourself for not being more on the ball. You cry when you drop something. You bark at your husband. In the midst of all this, you may not realize that lack of sleep is at the center of the chaos. Sleep-deprived people are prone to mood swings and feelings of inadequacy—as though parenting doesn't give you enough of those on its own! Without enough sleep you can also be irritable and lethargic, crave sweets, and suffer from burning eyes.

When I was expecting and celebrating new babies, I swore I'd hurl the next book that told me to "sleep when baby sleeps." Who was going to pay bills, return phone calls, write thank-yous, make dinner?—you get the picture. Many women, especially those who have left behind careers for motherhood, long to feel productive and high functioning, so they sacrifice sleep for getting that one more thing done. Personally, I also hated being wakened from a nap by a crying baby. I always felt groggy and out of whack for at least an hour after—worse, I reasoned, than if I'd not slept at all. By my third child, I learned how essential naps were and how overrated our personal-need productivity is.

Yes, naps are going to be interrupted, but they are crucial to recovering from ragged nights of disconnected sleep. You can't erase a sleep debt with naps, but you can gradually diminish its effects. For decades researchers have been telling us that

The Yawn of a New Day
Maximizing Your Sleep

❋ When your baby dozes off, especially when he's full and freshly bathed, dive into bed. Don't waste time opening mail, unloading the dishwasher, or anything else. Every minute counts.

❋ Don't watch the clock as you fall asleep. That only increases anxiety and prevents good sleep.

❋ Watch your caffeine. You may need a jumpstart when you begin to fade during the day, but caffeine stays in your system longer than you think and interferes with the quality of your sleep. When nursing, limit caffeine to one or two eight-ounce servings per day. Caffeine in breast milk reaches its highest level one hour after you consume it and can cause irritability and poor sleep habits in babies.

❋ Resist the urge to play host to out-of-town guests. They are usually visiting to help, and that means letting you nap.

❋ Turn off the ringer on your phone when you are going to sleep.

❋ Turn down the monitor. Baby's breathing and gurgling can keep you alert and anxious when you are trying to recoup sleep. If the baby is in your room, consider napping in a different room.

❋ When you can, hand baby over to someone else just after a feeding, and then have that person use a bottle at the next feeding so you can spend the entire time sleeping. Longer periods of sleep can make a big difference.

❋ When you do hear baby, it's fine to wait a few minutes to see if she'll settle back down. You might both go back to sleep if you resist the urge to respond to every whimper. Many times a little fussing precedes settling back down.

children need a good night's sleep to learn. Parenting is the biggest education I've ever tried to attain. It makes sense that we need our sleep too.

The National Sleep Foundation says we need seven to nine hours of sleep for optimal performance. Sleep comes in four phases. The fourth phase is deep sleep, the rich stuff that lets your immune system do its job. Only after the first full sleep cycle is complete do we get to rapid eye movement or REM sleep, when we dream and process the day's stimuli. If you are wakened during any stage of the sleep cycle, it has to start over, so you miss that REM sleep and aren't giving your body the time it needs to adequately rest and your brain the time it needs to properly recharge.

There are logistical issues of sleep deprivation and emotional ones too. The cycle of feeding, diapering, and loving a baby becomes a twenty-four-hour cycle in the blink of an eye. As new parents, you find the day just doesn't stop anymore. You'll be feeding the baby and notice the sun rising, and you'll long powerlessly to stop it. The day has started—or did it never end?

Several of my friends, as they looked lovingly and bleary-eyed at their new babies, have had others tell them: "You are going to be tired for the rest of your life." At first that seems hopeless and insensitive. But parents of toddlers to teens concur that it's in part true—your sleep patterns change as a parent, whether you are getting little ones a drink in the middle of the night, are up with sick kids, or are waiting on teens to come home. "It's reassuring," one friend told me, "that I'm not doing something wrong. It just is what it is. You sleep less once you have kids." Once you accept that there's a new normal to your sleep patterns, you can go about making the most of what you can get.

The Mayo Clinic and many experienced parents recommend keeping consistent bedtimes for you as well as your baby. Go ahead and get pajamas on, brush your teeth, calm the house in preparation for bed—at a regular time—even though in your mind you might be preparing for a wakeful night with a newborn. Going through the routine will help your internal biological clock, which in turn will help you get the best sleep you can when you do sleep.

I asked my husband what he thought about our sleep deprivation learning curve. He said we just learned how not to stress or take it out on each other as we realized it was a temporary state. He also said, "The first good night of sleep we got after Zach was the night we left the monitor off by mistake." So true. We nicknamed our son "Barnyard" that first year because he sounded like every animal in the farm—awake or asleep. He got through that no-monitor night all by himself. What a concept for a new parent! I'm not endorsing turning your monitor off, but you may want to consider how loud you are keeping it and how instantly you respond to each peep baby makes.

We did learn something else just as inadvertently. When you are trying to sort out the reasons your baby is wailing in the night, you can barely open your eyes, and your husband asks what's wrong with the baby, in most cases he is not saying, "You are an unfit mother. I really want to go back to bed. Can't you figure this out?" Even if that's what you hear. He is simply wanting to help all three of you get back to bed. Marital snapping in the wee hours is normal. It's not pretty, and you should definitely try to refrain, but it's normal. Let it go, and pledge to do better the next night.

As I mentioned, being wakened by crying was hard for me. I find being wakened by *anyone* fairly unpleasant. To avoid feeling as though this were happening several times a night, I tried sleeping on the couch when I first "went to bed" around 9 p.m. That way, when baby woke for the midnight feeding, I felt more like I'd had a good nap than a bad night's sleep. I'd go to my own bed after that, and

"I remember being on the phone with my aunt, **and I just started** bawling. We were talking about nothing— maybe the outfit she sent—and I just had to hand over the phone. **It didn't seem** normal, **but my mom made it seem** fine. She knew."

Stacia

"I don't know why there's such a stigma to taking an antidepressant. It's not like it's tattooed on your forehead. It **doesn't mean you are a failure.** You just have a chemical imbalance, maybe for a while, maybe forever. **I used to say, 'No thanks, I'll be fine.'** And my husband finally said, 'You can't do this anymore. It's not good for you or Hanna.' I just know I never want to feel like that again. It's the worst feeling in the world."

Sara

with one more feeding at 3 a.m., I felt as though I'd just been wakened once. It was a mental game, but I was tired enough to sleep anywhere with my own pillow, and it worked for me.

The couch trick had some other implications too. When I was on the couch, I didn't have to worry about disturbing my husband by turning on the TV. I kept the room dark and the volume low for both baby and me, but focusing on something helped me stay awake. I learned to love catching up on some recorded TV—thank you, digital age—and even sometimes planned to watch something special, so it would be easier not to resent having to be awake. Some women I know did every night feeding in dark silence. When I had the company of the TV, I felt more intentional about middle-of-the-night mealtimes instead of feeding my sons like a reluctant zombie.

Many women have a hard time staying awake in the middle of the night while feeding a baby, and there were times when I'd feed the baby with my eyes at half-mast, hoping to somehow keep the sleep vibe going. Then I'd jerk awake wondering how long I had been dozing, with no idea if the baby had eaten well or fallen asleep himself. Several women I know used a little timer for their night feedings, so if they did doze off, they'd wake up and know how long baby had nursed. I wish I'd thought to try that. Bottle feeding is a little different in that babies might gag or take in unnecessary air if you aren't watching carefully. If you are bottle feeding, make sure you have everything ready for a quick nighttime bottle. Why turn on the lights to measure powder at 3 a.m. if you don't have to? Do what works for you, don't hesitate to ask others what's worked for them, and never be afraid to change up your routine if it's *not* working.

My friend Lynette found watching TV during a night feeding frustrating. She was too tired to focus. Also she couldn't find comfort in the overnight quiet of the house. "I remember actually dreading the night coming," she said, "until I finally brought the baby to bed."

Co-sleeping, as it's called, is the source of much debate. Opponents say it's stressful and dangerous. Advocates say it promotes bonding, breast-feeding, and better sleep. It would take more than this entire book to report the full debate and research on the subject. Do your homework on this issue and talk to your pediatrician. I never trusted myself or my husband not to roll over on baby.

Lynette admits she took her baby to bed out of desperation and against what she had read. But as an immobile sleeper, she said it gave her not only the rest she needed but her first experience in using her intuition to do what she felt was best for her family, despite varied advice. Whatever you do at night, do it safely. There are several products that seek to make co-sleeping safer, including side rails—enclosures you place around the baby directly on your bed—and three-sided bassinettes that attach to the side of an adult bed.

Again, being tired can make you edgy. Consider sleep deprivation a key ingredient to the emotional stew that bubbles about after having a child. But it's important to realize there could be something else cooking.

The Fog

I think I used to wear sleep deprivation as some twisted badge of courage. Whenever my babies needed me, I was going to be there. But my second son was small, and his little tummy couldn't get him through the night without one or more feedings for months and months and months.

In retrospect I can see that I was increasingly edgy and my patience was disappearing. My husband had been traveling a lot, and I remember standing at the kitchen counter, making some

What to Look For

Any of these symptoms after pregnancy that last longer than two weeks may be signs of postpartum depression:

- Feeling restless or irritable
- Feeling sad, hopeless, and overwhelmed
- Crying a lot
- Having no energy or motivation
- Eating too little or too much
- Sleeping too little or too much
- Having trouble focusing, remembering, or making decisions
- Feeling worthless and guilty
- Lacking interest in the baby
- Losing interest or pleasure in activities
- Withdrawing from friends and family
- Having headaches, chest pains, heart palpitations (the heart beating fast and feeling like it is skipping beats), or hyperventilation (fast and shallow breathing)
- Being afraid you might hurt the baby or yourself

If you're experiencing any of these symptoms over an extended period of time, be sure to consult your physician.

National Women's Health Information Center, U.S. Dept. of Health and Human Services, www.4women.gov

excuse of a meal for dinner, thinking that if my life was a flavor that day it would be sugar-free vanilla. Bland, void, empty. I wondered where the joy had gone. And then I wondered what would cause such an ungrateful thought after the birth of a happy baby. I would talk to friends on the phone but wouldn't really want to be engaged in conversation. And then one such friend asked if I'd talked to my OB lately.

I was still clueless.

Another friend, who had suffered from post-partum depression, saw the signs that I was sinking. I got a little teary on the phone for no reason I could pinpoint. She insisted I pack up the kids and meet her family at McDonald's for dinner within the hour. On arrival, her intuitive husband snatched the baby and a bottle from me. As I watched him smile and ga-ga at my precious boy, I realized something was wrong with me. I adored my kids, but I had lost my own ga-ga.

I called the doctor and welled up just trying to explain why I needed an appointment. By now I knew something was up. When I sat on the exam table, I eyed a purple flier on the wall: the signs of postpartum depression. There I was—my life, hanging on the wall. It had been there for nine months of prenatal appointments, and I'd read it before. And I *still* hadn't recognized what was happening to me. I turned a corner that very moment, knowing finally that I had been living in a fog, and the fog had a name. I was familiar with the term "baby blues," but depression was completely foreign to me. I got down once in a while, but I had to *try* to stay down. I was proud of that. I always bounced back up. I was a floater.

But I'd never been a woman with two kids, a traveling husband, and less than four hours connected sleep each night for five months. I never realized sleep deprivation exacerbates postpartum depression. I thought postpartum depression came

Emotions in Motion

Taking Care of Yourself

- Get as much rest as you can.

- Try not to spend too much time alone.

- Spend some time alone with your husband.

- Ask for help caring for your baby.

- Keep a diary. Write down your feelings as a way of "letting it all out." Rereading it later will help you see how much better you are.

- Exercise for better sleep and a better self-image.

- Take a shower and get dressed.

- Do something you enjoy every day, out of the house if you can, even for just fifteen minutes.

- Be gentle with yourself. Don't aim for an immaculate house.

- Talk to other mothers about their experiences.

on quickly after childbirth, not five months later. And I would soon be stunned at how many of my friends—good friends—had been through something similar, and I'd never known.

Perhaps women don't talk about the range and severity of their emotions after having a child because they're not sure what's normal. They are embarrassed—even though postpartum depression can be one of the most common complications of childbearing. You hear of a few high-profile cases but you don't know where your own story fits in. And you try to tell yourself it doesn't.

The Forecast

Here's what's happening physically. During pregnancy, the hormones estrogen and progesterone increase greatly in a woman's body. After having a baby, these hormones take a rapid dive that researchers think may lead to depression—just as small hormonal fluctuations can change our mood before a menstrual period. There have been studies that support a group of other issues—history of depression, fatigue, marital strife, social support, financial support—as the roots of post-baby depression in women, as well as in men.

The baby blues occur a few days to a few months after giving birth but can make a comeback later in baby's first year due to mom's stress or sleep deprivation. New moms may feel sad, overwhelmed by new responsibilities, irritable, or restless; they may cry often and perhaps have that sense of disappointment we spoke of earlier. Being alone, single, or away from family and the care of nurses can bring on anxiety or fear. The blues, which are thought to affect up to 80 percent of new moms, usually resolve themselves without any treatment within a week or so. Napping when the baby does and reaching out to others can help.

If you've left the work world, for the foreseeable future or a limited maternity leave, this emotional adjustment adds another dimension. Personally, I was incredibly ready to stay home after years of trying to have children, but still I missed the daily interaction with co-workers, feedback on my performance, and having a clear idea of what the day's goals were.

"You lose some of your identity, going from an atmosphere where people know you to being at home changing diapers. It pulls on your heart," Lynda said. "I wish I'd thought more realistically about that before I had my daughter."

Postpartum depression may at first seem like a case of the blues, but it differs in severity. It begins in the first two to three months after childbirth, depletes a mom's pleasure or interest in life, and keeps women from functioning well for longer than a couple weeks as with the blues. It goes deeper than the blues and can feel paralyzing. Estimates vary—

and many women are never formally diagnosed—but studies have shown up to 20 percent of moms experience postpartum depression.

"I feel like, after a few years, I can now differentiate between a little fog and a big cloud," says my friend Kelly. "If I felt something, and then felt extreme guilt, it was depression, not just the blues."

Kelly learned the hard way. She was surprised by the instant shift in focus from her to her new son. She had a difficult time nursing and finding help, and she started doubting her ability to be a good mom. Her self-esteem lagging, she started to withdraw.

"I remember sitting in a rocker feeding my son and looking outside at a neighbor mom who had three kids between six and thirteen. They were coming back from a soccer game. I was thinking, *I hate this point in my life. I wish I could fast-forward to* that. And then I wondered what was

factors that contribute to developing
Postpartum Depression

- Having experienced major depression in the past
- A history of hormonal problems, such as PMS
- Difficulty conceiving or repeated pregnancy losses (something that can boost your expectations of parenthood extremely high)
- Delivering your baby prematurely or by C-section
- Giving birth to more than one baby
- Having either a very big or small gap between pregnancies
- Experiencing marital stress
- Feeling isolated or lonely at home
- Lacking family support
- Having experienced the death of a parent during childhood or adolescence

wrong with me. I cried a lot during the day, home alone, never around my husband. I kept thinking, *I'm not even working; how can I not be happy and have this mom thing under control?"*

For six months she blamed her feelings on being tired. Kelly did start to show her emotions to her husband, bawling as he got ready to leave for work, knowing that she faced another day of "sinking." He'd suggest she call the doctor, and she'd just feel more inadequate and embarrassed. Sharing the warning signs of postpartum depression with your husband or a family member is important, since they might be more in tune to warning signs you are exhibiting than you are.

Kelly wasn't aware she had something else working against her. She suffered "a little depression" during her first semester in college when her parents divorced. Previous depression is among the factors that make women more susceptible to postpartum woes. Having had postpartum depression also increases the chances you'll have it again. I know with my next child, I was looking for it.

Clearing Skies

So you think you know what's going on. Now what do you do? See your doctor, soon. One tool to assess your symptoms is the Edinburgh Postnatal Depression Scale, a simple, ten-item question-naire about what you've experienced in the previous seven days. A simple blood test may also be in order. Sometimes the level of your thyroid hormones is low after childbirth. The thyroid is a gland in your neck that helps regulate how your body uses and stores energy from food, otherwise known as your metabolism. When your thyroid is off, you may get depression symptoms like irritability, fatigue, and difficulty concentrating.

My dear friend Sara had a six-month-old when she started feeling anxious and panicky. "It was like

"I cried a lot, and I was tired.

I couldn't get a grasp on my life.

I wasn't sure of my identity anymore.

I felt inadequate immediately
after she was born,

but it carried over until she was about eight months.

My husband came home from work one day,

and I was still in my pj's. He said, 'Get dressed.

We're going for a walk.' I think joining

MOPS (Mothers of Preschoolers)

saved my life. It was a reason to get dressed,

a place to go, a purpose, a way to serve.

I was needed. It wasn't that I was shy.

I was just alone."

Lisa

I'd had five hundred cups of espresso," she said. "I didn't want to be alone and I remember having a full-blown panic attack in Hobby Lobby."

A doctor visit found her thyroid was indeed low. But medication, which takes four to six weeks to effect change, didn't take the edge off.

"I thought I was going to crawl out of my skin," she said. "I can vividly remember thinking when I put my daughter to bed, *I'm going to die in my sleep tonight*."

It turned out Sara's thyroid wasn't just low but fluctuating, so medication caused her symptoms to worsen. She was also diagnosed with and given medication for postpartum depression. Her experience underscores the importance of following through on doctor visits and blood tests, even though at a given moment, you might think you're feeling better.

Rest, exercise, and good nutrition can help the symptoms of postpartum depression; so can joining

The Perfect

My friend Jamie's picture should be next to the word *joy* in the dictionary. She has an infectious smile and a belly laugh for any situation, especially when it relates to parenting.

Her personality is all the more magnetic when you learn that it was molded through surviving postpartum psychosis, a disorder affecting one or two women in one thousand births.

In her third trimester, Jamie found herself on a sickening roller coaster, laughing uncontrollably and full of passion in the same day that she'd spend four hours crying uncontrollably on her bed. Days of labor, a colicky son, a lack of family support, and a husband with just three days off from work for a new baby combined for "a perfect storm of badness," as Jamie called it.

Jamie's husband, Jason, watched his wife disappear, though her body remained. Without shame she recounts what happened three weeks after having her son: "He cried all day. I cried all day. I wondered who made who cry. I called my husband and told him I wanted to jump out the window and throw the baby out the window too. He rushed home and saw I was sitting by the window, with makeup running down my face. I had actually put makeup

Storm...

on that day because I told myself this was the day I'd stop being sad. This was the day I'd get it together."

Jamie's case of the most severe postpartum mood disorder was textbook, coming on two to three weeks after delivery and bringing with it such symptoms as hallucinations and delusions, illogical thoughts, insomnia, refusing to eat, periods of delirium or mania, suicidal or homicidal thoughts, and extreme feelings of anxiety and agitation.

Jamie was put on major medication and saw a psychiatrist and psychologist weekly, inching her way through her son's first year. Her doctor told her she shouldn't have more children because of her family's history of the illness and the risk of suffering even more severely the next time.

"You *can* get well again. There's such despair in being that ill, and I wish other women would talk about it. I wholly made the decision not to be embarrassed about it. To have to have your husband learn to trust you again with your own baby—that *is* embarrassing. But women need to share how hard being a mom can be, whatever they're feeling. You are supposed to love it but sometimes you don't. And you need to find and accept help.

"Motherhood is the most beautiful, painful process there is."

a support group or talking to a therapist, psychologist, or social worker.

Another option for many women is taking an antidepressant. It's a step some moms resist because they believe it says, "I can't do motherhood." It's just the opposite. If you had a bad headache that made you miserable and affected your ability to care for your new baby, you'd get help or try something like getting more rest. If that didn't work, you'd take something. You do what is needed to "do" motherhood.

The online postpartum support group says it so well:

Being a mother is one of the hardest jobs anyone can do, and having a mood disorder can make a hard job feel impossible. Many women experience some form of postpartum mood disorders. Having a mental illness is not a measure of your worth, social status, race, or religion. Getting treatment is not a sign of weakness, but a sign of strength and bravery.

Most women can expect to experience an improvement in postpartum symptoms within three months of starting treatment, and the majority will recover within a year. If you are doing well but another new mom you know isn't, don't pull away from her. Be there for her. You may be able to help her find and hold fast to perspective, which is so important. If you can't see the light at the end of the tunnel—and you're in the middle of the tunnel—it's hard to believe the end exists and that you will not always feel like you're in the shadows.

Your Body after Baby
Babying Me

1. Am I getting all the sleep I can? What could help my ability to rest?

2. What has surprised me about my emotions?

3. Do I have a friend or family member I'm able to talk honestly with about my feelings? Am I hiding any feelings from my husband?

4. What are my perceptions of depression?

Daddy Dish

A New Day for Both of You

A friend told me the story of her husband going out with friends not long after she'd been through a difficult delivery. He had the chance to relax and have a few beers while his mom was in town to help support his wife and new baby. On his way home, he pulled over to the side of the road and sobbed. He too had experienced a life-changing event and needed a release.

"It made me feel good that he was feeling things so deeply too," she said. "I think I'd been discounting a little what he'd been through."

I know I've never watched anyone—let alone someone I loved enough to marry—endure pain that made him or her scream out. I've never been dressed in scrubs, inches away from where they are doing surgery on my spouse to introduce my new baby to the world. While there is plenty my husband can't grasp about being a mom, there's just as much I can't claim to know about being a dad.

When it comes to understanding your mind and body after having a baby, men can't. After all, *we* don't fully understand our *own* minds and bodies, right? So while we are enduring so many of the physical and mental repercussions of childbirth, we have to make sure we provide windows for dad to peer through.

I'm not suggesting you alert him to every time you gush blood or have a milk letdown. I said windows, not garage doors. But encourage him to read the post-baby literature from the hospital, especially the C-section recovery recommendations if you've had one. Set aside "couch time" every day, allowing no interruptions, to touch base on how each of you is doing with your new world order. If there is something he *can* do to help, ask him. He cannot read your mind.

Men can find a woman's emotional aftershocks from giving birth particularly hard to deal with. Imagine if *he* were crying at the drop of a hat and all you could see was an innocent little infant at the root of it all. He hasn't lost anything from inside his body. He's gained something—his first tangible look at and feel of the role he assumed nine months ago. And, like you, he's gained a lifelong responsibility overnight.

As the love of my life says, "Even the perfect husband can't help postpartum. You can't fix it and you don't want to make her feel worse by suggesting there's something wrong with her. You're between a rock and a hard place." Todd says that knowing about the reality of the blues and depression was key to not urging me to take a mind-over-matter approach to dealing with it. I wouldn't have taken well to that. So make sure your husband knows the warning signs of postpartum depression. His clear mind can help when yours is on leave.

Stay close to your husband physically and emotionally, even though your mind and body may feel less than lovable. Maintaining intimacy may look different as your body heals and you begin integrating a child into your home, but it's even more important to your marriage now. (Another book in this series, *The New Mom's Guide to Dealing with Dad*, offers much more on staying connected to your spouse.)

With a new baby at home, resuming your sex life may be the last thing on your mind, or it could be a fairly dominant thought, especially if those last months of pregnancy were uncomfortable and sex was off limits. You may be anxious for a familiar intimacy to balance the many changes in your life. I'll bet your husband is.

Many doctors recommend waiting six weeks before resuming intercourse, though of course some couples do not wait that long. When your bleeding has stopped, any tearing has healed, and your vaginal area is comfortable again, it's usually fine to have sex. The six-week checkup is an ideal time to put your mind at ease and a sensible milestone to work toward. That said, if you are ready sooner, talk to your doctor. You want to avoid additional bleeding or introducing infection, and if you've had a C-section, you must guard against undue stress on the incision.

It's quite likely sex won't feel the same. Think about all that your body has been through. The muscle tone in the vagina could be decreased, and that can decrease your ability to be aroused, at least for a while. Kegel exercises, done by tightening your muscles as if you're trying to stop a stream of urine, can tone your pelvic floor muscles. You may also be dry and tender and should consider a vaginal lubricant to make sex more comfortable. Go slowly, and don't be frustrated if the first time or so isn't your idea of ideal.

Don't forget birth control. Many a surprising conception has happened in the months after having a baby, whether the woman was nursing or not. Birth control is definitely something to check in with your doctor about at your six-week visit.

You might be thinking, *How in the world is anyone thinking about sex right after having a baby?* Plenty of women are with you there.

"I felt like a cow," Denise said. "I'd had doctors touching and poking me, and I'm a very modest person. Having that first baby was traumatizing, and for a long time it was uncomfortable having sex. But keeping emotional and physical intimacy is something you need to do. It will fill *your* tank too."

It's extremely important to nurture your marriage physically—whether it's through sex, hugs and kisses, or holding hands. Talk about your needs, where your body is in healing and dealing with your new world. Consider different times of day for intimacy if bedtime becomes a weary blur. Freshen up with a soothing shower and fresh nightie. Feed the baby before you rendezvous to give yourselves plenty of time.

Even though sex may not sound appealing, you might be very glad you went ahead and made love. Or you may talk about some other ways to satisfy either of you sexually if you simply aren't ready for intercourse. Sometimes moms live in their heads, but leading with your heart and body can be very rewarding.

These months after having a baby are indeed like riding a roller coaster. Sometimes you want to grab the hand of the person you're riding with, to scream and laugh together. Other times you want to dump your fear and nerves on your spouse. Be gentle with one another, but do *be* with one another. The ride will even out. And sharing both the thrills and chills, well, that's what makes a family a family.

Your Body after Baby
Babying Me

1. How is my husband doing emotionally? Have I asked him?

2. Have I shared my feelings of depression with my husband?

3. What three things can I do to develop emotional intimacy with my husband?

4. Where am I with physical intimacy? Have my husband and I discussed resuming our sex life?

Happy
Mothering

Embracing Your New You

Whether this is your first or fifth baby, the time after a child is born is one of heightened sensitivities and change. There's a new person in your house, and I'm not talking about your baby. You are not the person you were before you brought this little person into the world, but you can emerge from these months a better woman, an undoubtedly stronger one. The best is yet to come.

Happy mothering. Happy babying *you*.

Acknowledgments

From Susan

Thank you to the dozens of women who shared with me their ups and downs, moments of great triumph and great disgust, and the yearning and yelling in their hearts. You elevate the calling of motherhood by your intense love, dedication, and authenticity.

MOPS has enhanced mothering around the world and now across generations. I am confident, and deeply grateful, that its ripple effects will be felt throughout my family tree. Beth Lagerborg, thank you for asking me to dwell with you in God's perfect timing.

Thank you to Dr. Monica Reed for reviewing this project for medical relevance and accuracy and for her dedication to women's health.

This book was possible because of women I love and was written for women I don't know, including the ones who will one day love my boys. Zach, Luke, and A.J., you are life's most amazing gifts and most humbling projects. Todd, your love inspires me. Our journey with them and with God is transforming my heart. Thank you for never giving up on my becoming a mom.

From Monica

I would like to acknowledge the team at MOPS International—Mary Beth Lagerborg, Carla Foote, and Jean Blackmer—who extended the opportunity to me to be involved in this wonderful "labor" of love; Lee Hough with Alive Communications—who continues to be an ardent supporter; and last but not least my husband, my children, and my God—all of whom make my life a wonder-filled adventure.

Susan Besze Wallace was a newspaper reporter for twelve years coast to coast, most recently with the *Denver Post*, before leaving to focus on the daily deadlines of sons Zach, Luke, and A.J. She led one of the largest MOPS (Mothers of Preschoolers) groups in the country and is a contributor to *MOMSense* magazine. Susan and husband Todd recently transplanted their busy brood to northern Virginia, where she continues writing freelance news stories and celebrating the roller coaster of motherhood in print.

Dr. Monica Reed is a physician, author, and speaker and has dedicated her life to promoting health, healing, and wellness. She currently serves as CEO of Florida Hospital Celebration Health. Dr. Reed is the author of *Creation Health Breakthrough: 8 Essentials to Revolutionize Your Health Physically, Mentally and Spiritually*. She and her husband Stanton Reed have two daughters: Melanie and Megan.

Better together...

MOPS is here to come alongside you
during this season of early mothering to
give you the support and resources you
need to be a great mom.

Get connected today!

Mothers of Preschoolers

2370 S. Trenton Way, Denver CO 80231
888.910.MOPS • **www.MOPS.org/bettermoms**

Perfect Gifts for a New Mom!

New moms run into a host of new challenges once baby arrives. *The New Mom's Guides* go straight to the heart of these matters, offering moms guidance and encouragement in this new season of life.